Vamos a ordenar/Sorting

Vamos a ordenar por Colores
Sorting by Color

por/by Jennifer L. Marks

Traducción/Translation: Dr. Martín Luis Guzmán Ferrer

Capstone press

Mankato, Minnesota

A+ Books are published by Capstone Press,
151 Good Counsel Drive, P.O. Box 669, Mankato, Minnesota 56002.
www.capstonepress.com

1 2 3 4 5 6 12 11 10 09 08 07

Library of Congress Cataloging-in-Publication Data
Marks, Jennifer L., 1979–
     [Sorting by color. Spanish & English]
     Vamos a ordenar por colores / por Jennifer L. Marks = Sorting by color / by Jennifer L. Marks.
     p. cm.—(A+ bilingüe. Vamos a ordenar = A+ bilingual books. Sorting)
     Includes index.
     ISBN-13: 978-1-4296-1196-1 (hardcover)
     ISBN-10: 1-4296-1196-0 (hardcover)
     1. Group theory—Juvenile literature. 2. Color—Juvenile literature. I. Title. II. Title: Sorting by color.
III. Series.
QA174.5.M3718 2008
512'.2–dc22   2007018451

Summary: Simple text and color photographs introduce basic concepts of sorting by color—in both English
     and Spanish.

Interactive ISBN-13: 978-1-4296-1130-5
Interactive ISBN-10: 1-4296-1130-8

Credits

Ted Williams, set designer; Kyle Grenz and Mary Bode, book designers; Katy Kudela,
     bilingual editor; Eida del Risco, Spanish copy editor; Charlene Deyle, photo
     researcher; Scott Thoms, photo editor

Photo Credits

Capstone Press/Karon Dubke, cover, 4–5, 6–7, 8, 9, 10–11, 12, 13, 14–15, 16, 17, 18,
     19, 20, 21, 22, 23, 24, 25
Shutterstock/Arturo Limon, 29; David Yuckert, 26; Diego Cervo, 28; Sasha Davas,
     27 (paint swatches); V. J. Matthew, 27 (towels)

Note to Parents, Teachers, and Librarians

The Vamos a ordenar/Sorting set uses color photographs and a nonfiction format to introduce readers to the
key math skill of sorting. *Vamos a ordenar por colores/Sorting by Color* in English and Spanish is designed to
be read aloud to a pre-reader, or to be read independently by an early reader. Images and activities encourage
mathematical thinking in early readers and listeners. The book encourages further learning by including the
following sections: Table of Contents, Venn Diagram, Facts about Color, Glossary, Internet Sites, and Index.
Early readers may need assistance using these features.

The author dedicates this book to her sister Rachel Marks of Mankato, Minnesota.

Table of Contents

Tabla de contenidos

So Many Shoes!

Look at this jumble
of colorful shoes!
How can we sort them?

¡Cuántos zapatos!

¡Mira esta mezcolanza de zapatos! ¿Cómo podemos ordenarlos?

Let's sort these shoes by color. We can make blue, pink, tan, and purple sets. A set is a group of alike things.

What else can we sort by color?

6

Podemos ordenar estos zapatos por colores. Podemos hacer grupos con los azules, los rosados, los marrones y los morados. Un grupo es un conjunto de cosas parecidas.

¿Qué otras cosas podemos ordenar por colores?

Sorting Food

A bag of fresh vegetables holds all kinds of crisp, tasty colors.

Una bolsa de verduras frescas contiene toda clase de colores frescos y sabrosos.

Vamos a ordenar los alimentos

Let's sort them into sets—green, orange, yellow, and purple.

Vamos a ordenarlas por grupos: verdes, anaranjadas, amarillas y moradas.

Yummy fruit can be
sorted by color too.
What three color sets
do you see here?

10

Las ricas frutas también pueden ordenarse por colores. ¿Qué tres grupos de colores puedes ver aquí?

11

Hungry for something even sweeter? Jellybeans are tiny but oh so tasty.

¿Se te antoja algo todavía más dulce? Los frijolitos de dulce son pequeñísimos pero qué sabor tienen.

12

Sort these sweets by color—red, orange, yellow, green, and blue.

Ordena estos dulces por colores: rojo, anaranjado, amarillo, verde y azul.

13

Toys and Games

Toys can be sorted by color too. These huggable teddy bears are sorted— white, black, and brown.

Juguetes y juegos

Los juguetes también pueden ordenarse por colores. Estos suaves ositos de peluche se han ordenado en blancos, negros y marrones.

15

The pegs are sorted by color. After each player chooses a set, the fun begins.

Las clavijas se ordenan por colores. Después de que cada jugador escoge un conjunto, la diversión empieza.

Arts and Crafts
Manualidades

Let's sort crayons by color. We'll make sets of orange, yellow, green, and blue.

Vamos a ordenar los crayones por colores. Hagamos grupos de anaranjados, amarillos, verdes y azules.

18

Why not sort your paints and brushes by color too?

¿Y por qué no ordenamos los pinceles también por colores?

It's lots of fun to press, pinch, and shape play dough into colorful creatures.

Es muy entretenido aplastar, pellizcar y darle forma a la plastilina para hacer criaturas llenas de color.

When you are done,
sort the dough by
color—green, yellow,
and pink.

Cuando termines,
puedes ordenar
la plastilina por
colores: verde,
amarilla y rosada.

21

Venn Diagrams/
Diagramas de Venn

Sometimes things can be sorted into more than one set. Let's use a Venn diagram to sort orange and blue shirts.

Algunas cosas también pueden ordenarse en más de un grupo. En un diagrama de Venn podemos ordenar unas camisetas anaranjadas y azules.

Blue

Azul

Blue and
Orange

Azul
y
anaranjado

Orange

Anaranjado

23

Fresh from the dryer, warm, fuzzy socks need to be sorted. Let's try another Venn diagram.

Recién salidos de la secadora los calcetines calentitos y peluditos tienen que ordenarse. Vamos a hacerlo en otro diagrama de Venn.

Pink

Rosado

Pink and Purple

Rosado y morado

Purple

Morado

25

Sorting by Color in the Real World

You can spot sorting in all kinds of places. Let's look at some of the ways people sort by color in the real world.

Tú puedes ver grupos ordenados en toda clase de lugares.

Red, yellow, orange, and green peppers are sorted by color in a grocery store.

Los pimientos amarillos, anaranjados, rojos y verdes se ordenan por colores en la tienda de comestibles.

Vamos a ordenar por colores en el mundo real

In department stores, towels are sorted by color. Shoppers can find just the color they need.

En las tiendas por departamentos, las toallas se ordenan por colores. Así los clientes pueden encontrar justo el color que quieren.

Stores that sell paint sort paint samples by color. The sorted samples make it easy for people to pick out the perfect color and shade of paint.

Las tiendas que venden pintura ordenan las muestras por colores. Ordenan las muestras para que les sea más fácil a las personas escoger el color y el tono perfectos de pintura.

Facts about Color

- The first Crayola crayons came in eight colors—black, blue, brown, green, orange, red, violet, and yellow. Today, there are more than 100 colors of crayons. To celebrate Crayola's 100th anniversary, four new colors were added in 2003—inch worm, jazzberry jam, mango tango, and wild blue yonder.

- Toothbrush companies, dentists, and the Massachusetts Dental Society all report that blue is the most popular toothbrush color in the United States.

- A little extra color can make food look even more delicious. Some food colors are made in laboratories. Others come from natural sources. Beets are often used to give pink lemonade its rosy color.

Datos sobre los colores

- Los primeros crayones Crayola venían en ocho colores: negro, azul, marrón, verde, anaranjado, rojo, violeta y amarillo. Hoy hay más de 100 colores de crayones. Para celebrar su aniversario número 100, se añadieron cuatro colores más en 2003: oruga geómetra, jalea de *jazzberry*, mango tango y azul del más allá.

- Las compañías que hacen pasta de dientes, los dentistas y la Massachussets Dental Society informan todas que el azul es el color preferido de cepillos de dientes en los Estados Unidos.

- Añadir un color puede hacer la comida aún más deliciosa. Algunos colores para los alimentos se hacen en los laboratorios. Otros son de origen natural. Las remolachas muchas veces se usan para darle a la limonada color rosada su tono rosado.

Glossary

Chinese checkers—a board game played with colored pegs or marbles

creature—a living being

crisp—firm and easily broken

jumble—a mix or disorganized pile

pinch—to squeeze with your thumb and index finger

set—a group of similar things

shade—the lightness or darkness of a color

Venn diagram—a kind of diagram that uses circles to show how things can belong to more than one set

Internet Sites

FactHound offers a safe, fun way to find Internet sites related to this book. All of the sites on FactHound have been researched byour staff.

Here's how:

1. Visit *www.facthound.com*

2. Choose your grade level.

3. Type in this book ID **1429611960** for age-appropriate sites. You may also browse subjects by clicking on letters, or by clicking on pictures and words.

4. Click on the **Fetch It** button.

FactHound will fetch the best sites for you!

Glosario

la criatura—ser viviente

las damas chinas—juego de mesa que se juega con canicas o clavijas de colores

el diagrama de Venn—tipo de diagrama a base de círculos que muestra cómo las cosas pueden pertenecer a más de un grupo.

fresco—firme y fácil de romper

el grupo—conjunto de cosas similares

la mezcolanza—mezcla o pila de cosas en desorden

pellizcar—exprimir con tus dedos pulgar e índice

el tono—lo claro u oscuro de un color

Sitios de Internet

FactHound te brinda una manera divertida y segura de encontrar sitios de Internet relacionados con este libro. Hemos investigado todos los sitios de FactHound. Es posible que algunos sitios no estén en español.

Se hace así:

1. Visita *www.facthound.com*

2. Elige tu grado escolar.

3. Introduce este código especial **1429611960** para ver sitios apropiados a tu edad, o usa una palabra relacionada con este libro para hacer una búsqueda general.

4. Haz un clic en el botón **Fetch It**.

¡FactHound buscará los mejores sitios para ti!

Index

Índice